Daniel's Journey

The Testimony of a Mother of "How God Showed Himself through the Journey"

Elizabeth Mgaya

ISBN 979-8-89130-897-8 (paperback)
ISBN 979-8-89130-898-5 (digital)

Christian Faith Publishing
832 Park Avenue
Meadville, PA 16335
www.christianfaithpublishing.com

In the book, the author has used imaginative names for the privacy and protection of the characters in the story. Any resemblance to actual persons, living or dead, is purely coincidental.

Contents

Introduction

The Power of Prayer

I can say with certainty that without prayers, Daniel would not be living today. During this journey, family and friends looked up to God, believing in a miracle. People of God in the US gathered online and in person in Tanzania, Sudan, and other places to cry out to God to heal Daniel.

I believe that this book will help anyone going through the challenges of life, regardless of the kind of challenge, to not lose hope. Keep your faith and believe that God is with you throughout the journey no matter how hopeless, hard, and painful the situation looks. He will bring His people to help you lift the burden.

I do not know how I survived this challenging and traumatic period and continued to push on if it weren't for faith. The journey is not over yet, but I believe that God is working on the full restoration of Daniel's health. He will never leave you nor forsake you, just hold onto Him.

I would like to thank my family, friends, and the family of God for standing with me throughout this journey. I cannot imagine this journey without all of you. I cannot mention everyone here because each one of you played a significant role in this journey. Allow me to give special thanks to my husband who took care of Daniel when I had to go back to work. I saw and continue to see God's favor, which I cannot fathom. Throughout the ten months that I was on leave of absence to be by my son's side, God provided for all our needs. I never worried about where the next support would come from.

We serve a living God. He is the same yesterday, today, and forever.

Daniel is very poor at communicating. I remember how I used to worry about him when he went to college in the United States. In the initial months, he would call or email often, and I was able to reach him easily. However, after a couple of months, I guess after he got used to college life and made friends, it was a struggle to reach him. I would call and leave messages, and he would not get back to me. In desperation, I would sometimes call his best friend, Charles, for him to convey a message to Daniel to call me back. When he called back, I would tell him that his silence worried me, and he would always say, "Mama, if I have any problem, you will be the first person to know."

On that fateful day, June 25, 2016, Daniel called me and said he had been hospitalized because of severe abdominal pains suspected to be kidney stones. Immediately, I consulted Dr. Google and learned that kidney stones could be treated easily and may not necessarily require surgical procedures. I was relieved to learn that, though I was still worried that my son was sick in the hospital by himself. In the meantime, I was calling and sending WhatsApp messages, checking how he was feeling, and encouraging him to rest. I asked him how long he thought they would keep him in the hospital, and he said he was not sure because it would all depend on his lab results. He was in pain, and they were giving him strong painkillers.

A couple of years back, Daniel had two knee surgeries, one in 2006 and the second one in 2013, and he navigated through it all without me being there. When he had the first surgery, he had assured me that he was fine and that his friends with whom he was living were taking good care of him. Oscar, Charles, and Raymond are friends with whom Daniel grew up in Addis Ababa, Ethiopia, when I was working there as a diplomat. Charles is Daniel's age, and they are very close friends. The second one happened when he had moved, and the same friends offered that he move in with them while he was recuperating, which he did. I thought this time around that I had to go and be with my son as the situation sounded more serious, and I thank God that I made that decision.

The following day, June 26, 2016, I was chatting via text with him, and he told me that they were going to put him under oxygen for a while to help him breathe because he had too much fluid in his lungs. I got confused and asked him where the fluid came from. I called him immediately, and he told me they had overloaded him with fluid and that he was having problems breathing; therefore, they were going to hook him on a ventilator to help him breathe. He said once he was on the ventilator, we would not be able to talk. I didn't know what a ventilator was then, but I figured this was something serious.

I was scared and confused because, before the ventilators, I thought the problem was straightforward, according to Dr. Google. I comforted him by telling him not to worry because God was in control and all would be well, and I also reminded him to pray. Then he told me, "Don't worry, Mom. I'm a strong guy." This was the last communication we had. After speaking to him that evening, I decided that I had to travel to the United States from Darfur, Sudan, the next day and be with my son. That same night, I packed my stuff ready to travel once I got permission from my supervisor.

My Travel to Kansas and God's Favor

The following morning, June 27, I went to the office and told my supervisor that I had an emergency and had to travel because my son was hospitalized. My heart was bleeding at the thought that he was lying in the hospital bed alone and that I was not there next to him. I thank God because my supervisor was very supportive and allowed me to travel.

Immediately, I booked my ticket to travel the same day and managed to do all the administrative procedures required before traveling. I went to the airport and checked in, and then one Sudanese security guy came and called me from the departure lounge and told me to get my hand luggage and follow him. I followed him, and he said that I was not manifested and therefore could not travel.

I informed him that I was traveling on an emergency and that my name had been added to the manifest, but he did not want to understand. I used all my contacts, and my colleagues in the office tried to help, but this guy did not budge. Mind you, I had to leave that afternoon because I was catching the Turkish Airlines flight from Khartoum early the next morning around one, so I could not afford not to travel.

Normally, there are commercial flights from Darfur to Khartoum, but unfortunately, they changed their schedule and were now leaving in the morning. Anyway, since it was God's plan for me to travel, I managed to travel that day. It was a miracle that I was able to travel because the authorities normally demand to get the passenger manifest twenty-four hours before the trip, but I was able to travel within sixteen to eighteen hours.

We arrived safely in Khartoum, and I took my flight to Istanbul, Turkey, then boarded for JFK, New York, and to my destination, Kansas. When I arrived at JFK, I transferred to LaGuardia Airport to catch my flight to Kansas. I had an eight-hour layover, but the weather was bad, so I ended up staying there longer. I felt like time was at a standstill, and I was tired and worried and just wanted to be with my boy.

I called the hospital a couple of times to check on Daniel. I had to speak with a nurse since I could not talk to him directly. My husband, Paul, was also calling the hospital and would update me on Daniel's condition every time he checked with the hospital.

While waiting at LaGuardia Airport, I saw "breaking news" on TV in one of the restaurants that there was an explosion at Istanbul International Airport, the airport I transited through about fifteen hours before. I was astounded, and I thanked God that I was not caught up in the saga and confusion that normally follow such incidents. The only thing I know is that if I had not left Darfur on June 27, I would have been caught up in the mess.

Finally, we left LaGuardia. I can't remember the exact time, but I arrived in Kansas around 1:00 a.m. on June 28. Daniel's aunt, Linda, and cousins Penny, Tom, baby Nancy, and Habib had arrived the evening before from Arkansas to come see him. They came to pick me up from the airport and took me directly to the Medical Center, where Daniel was hospitalized.

At the Medical Center

When we arrived at the hospital, we went into a building. Interestingly, all this time, I hadn't realized Daniel was in the ICU until we got to the hospital, even after talking to the nurses a couple of times and even during my conversation with Paul, it had not registered.

I believe God had blocked my ears from hearing the details and connecting the dots; otherwise, it would have been much tougher for me, and I would have worried more. We walked through the nurses' station, machines beeping all around, and I finally got to the room where my son was. I was shocked to see him hooked up to all sorts of machines; he was on life support. There were pumps pumping several medicines through the IV, the ventilator helping him to breathe as his lungs had collapsed, and all types of tubes, monitors, and cables on the side of the bed. I just couldn't hold myself. Tears filled my eyes, and I did not know what to do.

Seeing my son in that condition broke my heart. I wished I could take his pain and relieve him of the suffering. I could imagine how Mary, the mother of Jesus, felt witnessing her son being tortured and crucified (John 19:25). I felt like holding him in my arms, but there were too many tubes, needles, and cables around him, and I didn't know where to touch him. Linda tried to calm me down and comfort me. After a while, I managed to pull myself together. I knew that this was going to be a tough journey, but I had faith that it would come to pass. While in this pain, I heard a still, small voice telling me, "*This is for My glory.*" This is what kept me going and is still keeping me going to date because I believe that God had a reason for allowing this to happen.

In Daniel's room, there was a recliner and an armed chair. These became his aunt's and my bed. The room was crowded with all sorts of life support machines, making it difficult to maneuver around. One had to be careful not to unplug any of the tubes or cables. All one could hear were the machines beeping; machines monitoring his blood pressure, heartbeat, and oxygen level; the ventilator, you name it.

Nurses and respiratory and laboratory technicians would come in and out of the room to check his vitals and take blood samples for his labs. There was no dull moment. Despite all these commotions, we did not want to leave Daniel alone in the hospital. We stayed with him in his room and would go to his house to freshen up and come back to the hospital as soon as we could.

I would stretch on the recliner with my feet on the armed chair, while Linda would stretch on the armed chair with her feet on the recliner. It was not a comfortable position to sleep in, but we were satisfied because we were close to Daniel. Whenever we heard the machines beep, we would look up and see what was going on. When the nurses came in for something, we would be attentive to see what they were doing. In fact, there was no sleeping—maybe just dosing off.

Apart from his collapsed lungs, Daniel's temperature was very high and could not be controlled. They administered medication and put ice packs under his armpits and on the sides of his body to help control the temperature. Then on July 4, in the struggle to bring his temperature down, they decided to use a hypothermia blanket over him. That was another very difficult moment for me. Seeing my son covered under that green cooling blanket was heart-breaking. Around July 6, his kidneys packed up, and he was put on dialysis for four hours a day, six days a week. It was traumatizing for me and the family because Daniel's condition was getting worse instead of improving.

On July 11, at around 6:00 p.m., we were sitting with friends and family who had come to see Daniel. His nurse came to me and told me that Daniel's condition had changed drastically. I did not understand her because we were in the room a few minutes before and had just come out to talk with the visitors who had come to see him. She said they suspected that he had septicemia. I asked her how that could have happened because almost every day they took his blood to check for infection, and the infectious disease doctor kept assuring me that all the tests showed he had no infection. Also, they were administering him a lot of antibiotics to prevent any infection.

The friends who came to visit were stunned by the drastic change in Daniel's condition. I got up quickly and went to his room, and the nurses and respiratory technicians were frantically trying to save his life. He could not breathe even with the ventilator. They were now helping him to breathe manually with the oxygen bag. I was going in and out of the room, not knowing what to do. The commotion was so much, and the room was small.

Tess is a friend who worked with Daniel at Regional Medical Center. Seeing the situation, she decided to stay with Linda and me. My mind was racing. I cannot describe the state in which I was. I would go in to see my son, and there was nothing I could do. I felt so helpless.

At around 2:00 a.m., I asked what time the pulmonary doctor was coming to see my son, and when she called, I asked her to come over. She came and joined the team of nurses and respiratory technicians. They struggled to oxygenate Daniel, and it reached a stage where they gave up. It was like his body was rejecting the ventilator. At a certain point, his heart stopped, and they called "code blue" and resuscitated him.

We—Linda, Tess, and I—were sitting in the corridor just outside his room. After a while, the doctor came out and told us that there was nothing they could do and that Daniel was not going to make it through the night. They were even contemplating getting him off life support. God gave me extraordinary strength, and I told the doctor, "My son was going to make it, and she should go back and do what she was supposed to do."

The doctor went back, and after about fifteen minutes, one of the nurses came and told me the same thing, and I sent her back with the same response I gave the doctor. I must say that this nurse was very fond of Daniel. After another twenty minutes or so, a guy came. He was not a nurse or one of the medical personnel. He was the hospital superintendent and told us that if there were any family members we wanted to be around, we could call them.

I looked at Linda and Tess, then at him. I did not understand what he was driving at. We did not respond, and he left. I later came to know that he was the hospital superintendent. I thank God for the strength He gave me, like He has promised us in His word in Isaiah 40:29–31 because I believe that if I was not strong at heart and persistent with my actions, they would have unplugged the life support machines, and this would have been another story. But I believe it was not time for him to go yet.

It was a blessing that Tess stayed with us throughout the night because she is a nurse by profession. She was able to fill in Calvin over the phone on what was going on, and he provided advice on what to do. I cannot believe how I managed through those moments. Calvin is Daniel's uncle, who had come to see him a couple of days before July 12. He is a medical doctor, specializing in endocrinology. He had an opportunity to talk to all of Daniel's doctors to follow up on his progress and went through all his medical records, and he was convincingly satisfied with the care and optimistic that Daniel would get through this crisis.

That same morning, on July 12, after the doctors made their rounds, they told me that Daniel had to go in for surgery. I got confused because less than six hours before, they told me that my son was not going to make it, and now they were telling me that he had to go in for surgery because he had fluid in his abdominal cavity and that they did not know where it was coming from.

I did not know what to say or what to do. Tess was still with us, so she called Calvin to inform him that they were taking Daniel in for surgery. He asked to talk to the surgeon so that he could explain what was going on. After speaking to the surgeon, he told me that Daniel had to go for surgery because the doctors did not know what the fluid was and where it was coming from, and in some cases, it could be poisonous. He encouraged me and said we should leave everything in God's hands. "The Lord watches over you, the Lord is your shade at your right hand" (Psalm 121:5).

I did not have a choice but to agree with the decision and sign the authorization papers. To be frank, I did not expect that my son would come out of the operating room alive. Linda and I stayed in the waiting area of the operating room, and for the time being, we were quiet and did not talk much. Each of us was inundated with our thoughts. After an hour and a half or so, Daniel was wheeled out of the operating room and rolled back to the ICU. They moved him into a bigger room and had the dialysis machine moved in there. It was painful to see my son in such a condition.

Following the surgery, Daniel's body was swollen. You'd think he was going to burst. His body temperature was still very high; therefore, after the surgery, they did not put any clothes on him except for over his torso while the upper part of his body was uncovered. The room he was moved to was very cold. We could no longer sleep there with him, so we moved to the waiting room. Linda was worried that the way he was exposed to the cold might lead to pneumonia, but the nurses said that since his temperature was very high and they didn't want to give him medication to lower it to protect his liver, it was best to leave him like that. They assured us that he would not get pneumonia. After all, they were giving him a couple of very strong antibiotics.

After the surgery, Daniel stopped moving. Before the surgery, he would unconsciously move his legs and arms, even though they were restrained, frown, and the like, but now he was just there. Then Lynn, a good friend of Daniel, said to me, "Mom, how come they have removed the restraints they had on his arms?" I had not noticed that, but her being a nursing student picked it quite easily.

The next day, we asked his doctor, and he told us that during the surgery, they had a problem oxygenating him; therefore, he did not get enough oxygen to his brain, which resulted in him getting multiple strokes. He ordered a neurologist to come and evaluate him. She came and did some tests and referred the case to a neurosurgeon, saying that his brain was slow.

I did not get it. As a layperson, I did not expect his brain to be functioning normally because of his heavy sedation. The neurosurgeon did a CT scan and said there were fluids in his brain, and therefore, he recommended a procedure to drain the fluid. I could not believe what I was hearing. My son went into the hospital with severe abdominal pain, which was diagnosed as pancreatitis. Within twenty-four hours, his lungs collapsed, and a couple of days later, his kidneys failed, his liver had issues, and now his brain had fluid. Things were getting more complicated and confusing.

I went outside the hospital to get some fresh air, and I cried my heart out. I called my husband, Paul, while crying uncontrollably. I believe I scared him. I explained what was happening, and he comforted me, assuring me that all would be well. At that stage, as a family, we decided to move Daniel from the hospital. We couldn't stand another piece of bad news.

As God would have it, Daniel's cousin, Dylan, had come from Ohio to see him. He pushed for us to move Daniel, but remember, he was on life support, and the doctors and the hospital were saying they could not take the risk of releasing him because he could not make it without being hooked on the ventilator.

Before Daniel got sick, he was working at a Regional Medical Center as a CNA. We asked the hospital administration to call the Regional Hospital, and they were ready to receive him, so they prepared everything that was required. He was removed from the ventilator and put in the ambulance with an oxygen mask. Dylan rode with him in the ambulance.

We took a risk, but for our sanity, it was the best thing to do at the time.

God went before us, and everything was set for him, and he arrived safely. This was after three weeks in the Medical Center. Ideally, the ventilator was supposed to be removed from the mouth and put through his trachea after fourteen days to avoid infection of the lungs.

During his stay at the Medical Center, friends and family were very supportive throughout this period. The community of young Tanzanians and Kenyans took good care of Linda, me, and the guests who came out of state to visit. They brought us food and made sure we were comfortable in the hospital. We got the support of friends who have now become family.

Max and Irene, his fiancée, were there for us too. Max would be the one picking up the visitors coming out of state from the airport. It was such a blessing to have them all rally around us during these trying times. I remember one day when Enid had promised to bring us fruits to the hospital, and when she got home that evening, she received bad news that her mom had passed away in Tanzania. The following day, despite the grief, she still made sure she brought the fruits to the hospital. I could not comprehend such a kind of love.

During this time, we were blessed by family members visiting from out of state. Daniel's aunt Judy and sister-in-law Rita visited from Columbus, Ohio. My cousin Anthony visited from North Carolina, and Daniel's cousin Dylan from Columbus, Ohio, and friends from Missouri and Colorado. Of course, my husband and my younger son would come and go to support us whenever they got an opportunity.

At the hospital, there was a chapel close to the ICU where I would retreat for prayers. To be frank, most of the time, I couldn't pray. Sometimes I would sing in my heart the song "Way Maker" by Sinach. This was my comforting song and the Bible scripture from Philippians 4:6–7.

ELIZABETH MGAYA

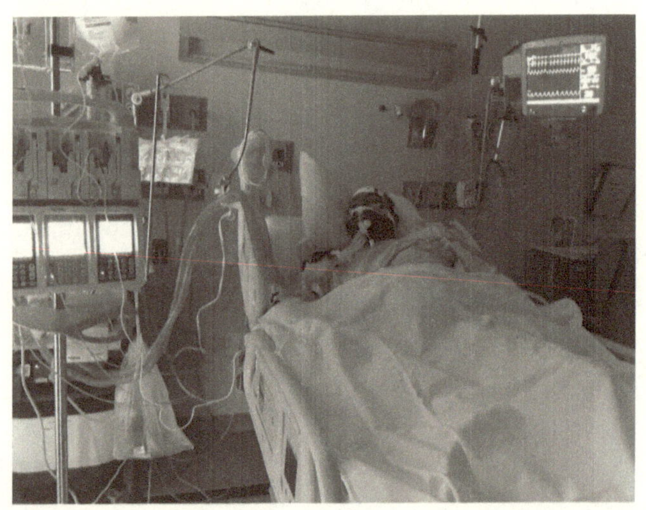

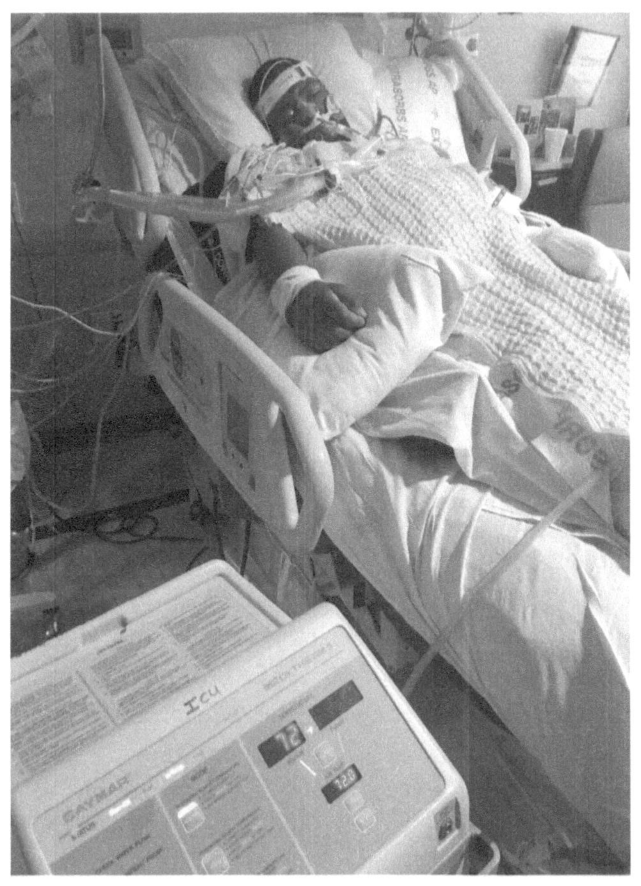

At the Regional Medical Center

On July 16, when he arrived at the Regional Medical Center, they were prepared to receive him, and he was sent directly to the ICU and hooked onto the life support machines. Doctors with different specialties were waiting for him and immediately did all the necessary examinations and tests. Two days later, on July 18, they tracked him and ventilated him through the trachea. They did another CT scan and did not see the need for the procedure that the neurosurgeon at Medical Center had recommended. Daniel was still not responding—no movement at all. He remained in the same position until it was time for the nurses to reposition him, which was every two hours. He continued with dialysis six days a week for four hours daily. It was an aggressive measure meant to revive his kidneys. His body was still swollen, and he had monitors monitoring his oxygen levels, heartbeat, and blood pressure. He was still on strong antibiotics and seductive medications, which were administered intravenously.

Linda and I continued to stay in the hospital. Again, we found a corner in the waiting/visitor's room where we settled, sleeping on recliners. Friends and family visiting from out of state would join us, as we were permanently at the hospital. As previously, we would just go to Daniel's house to freshen up and come back. We were blessed that we did not have to worry about food because God had sent His angels, who continued to take care of us.

Daniel's condition was not showing much improvement. He still had high temperatures, and his body was swollen. Additionally, his surgical wound continued to ooze fluid, and the doctors could not tell where this was coming from. Therefore, on July 22, the doctors decided to perform another surgery.

You will recall that the first surgery was done ten days earlier to remove whatever fluid was in his abdominal cavity, and tubes were inserted to drain the fluid coming from the cavity into bulbs that collect the fluid. The surgeon at the Regional Medical Center told me they removed about 2.5 liters of fluid and that his abdominal cavity was covered with gray and brown membranes. They did not know what exactly those were, and as a result, during the procedure, they could not go in further as they were cautious not to perforate or puncture his intestines or other internal organs. They used a temporary wound closure method as they felt that they may need to do another procedure. A third procedure was performed on July 24, again to drain the fluid and clean the abdominal cavity, after which they decided to irrigate the abdomen to ensure that the heavy fluid was drained out.

Again, on July 26, Daniel went for the fourth surgery. This time, the surgeon was satisfied that the fluid was reducing, and he closed the wound. You can imagine undergoing four surgeries within sixteen days. All this time, Daniel was unconscious and was in the ICU. I still do not know how I survived this rollercoaster of overwhelming emotions if not for God. He has promised us in Isaiah 41:10 that He will strengthen and help us and will uphold us with His righteous right hand. His body was still bloated, his temperatures were high, and he was still on dialysis.

While all this was going on, he contracted C. diff, a hospital-acquired disease. The situation was bad in the ICU. Almost all the patients contracted it. Since C. diff is highly contagious, everyone going into the patient's room was required to gown up and wear gloves. It was a pity that patients who were already in serious condition had to endure such a horrible infection.

The aggressive dialysis helped, and after about five weeks, Daniel's kidneys started to function. The fluid in his body was decreasing, and his body started to slowly shrink. Glory to God.

One thing that surprised me was how our bodies behave when we do not use them. His skin was peeling and his feet and hands were cracked like dryland, so we used to massage them with olive oil and warm water every two to three days.

The afternoon before we moved from the Regional Hospital to the Specialty Hospital, Christine, Max's mother; Timon, Max's brother; and children; Grace; Oscar, his wife, and children came to visit us at the hospital. These are the families we lived with in Addis Ababa. It was always comforting to see friends come to visit. I felt so blessed though sometimes it would bring emotions as it would bring back past memories.

While at the Regional Hospital, we were visited by family members coming out of state to empathize with us—my aunt Mary, cousin Bessie, Sheila, Daniel's cousin Damian, and his son Elias, Matt, Yolanda, Prince, and Paul. Friends living in Kansas continued to visit and bring food, drinks, and whatever they felt we would need.

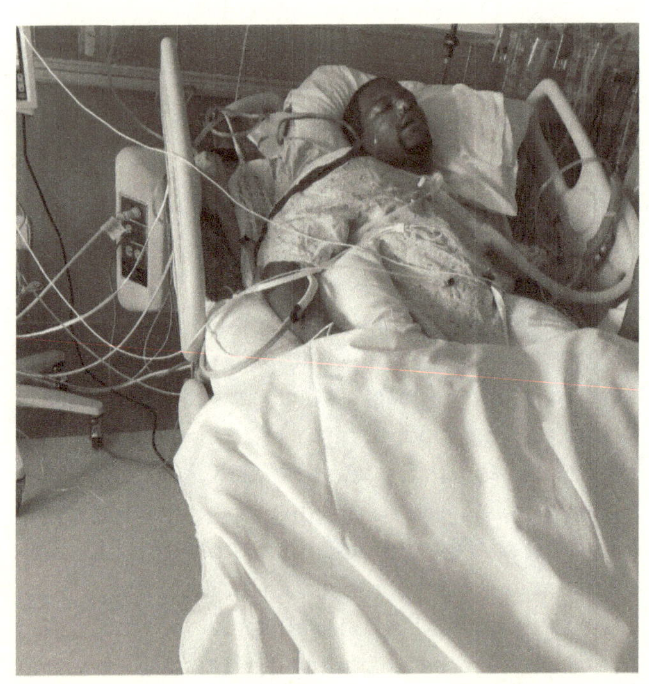

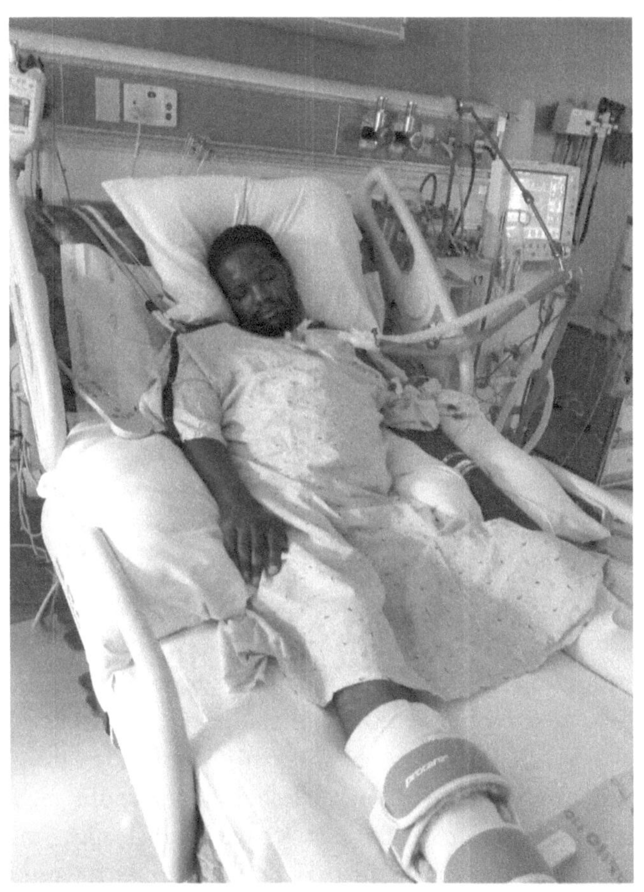

The Specialty Hospital

After seven weeks in the Intensive Care Unit, it was time for Daniel to be transferred to a more specialized hospital. The case manager was very helpful; she contacted several facilities and settled for the acute care specialized Hospital. She contacted the facility, and their PR came to meet me and talk to me about the hospital. Before we moved Daniel, Harry and Doreen went with me to see the place. We were met by one of the nurses on duty, and he took us around the place and showed us the room they had prepared for Daniel. It was a private room with an en suite bathroom. We asked if I could stay with Daniel, as I wouldn't want to be away from him. He said it was okay, and then Doreen asked if they could get a sleeping cot for me because I have been sleeping on recliners, and they said they could arrange for one. She also requested that we bring a refrigerator where I could keep the food all the friends would bring.

Doreen and friends bought the fridge so that I would be able to store food because the hospital we had moved to was a distance from where most of the friends were, and they could mostly visit on weekends, except for Doreen and Harry, who were closer.

On the afternoon of August 16, Daniel was moved to the acute care Specialty Hospital, where he would be weaned from the ventilator. Tess and Max helped Daniel and me move to the Specialty Hospital. Daniel and I rode in the ambulance, while Tess and Max helped move our belongings. God continued to shower us with His blessings by using His people to comfort and support us.

Daniel was still not conscious, but most of the machines and needles had been removed, except for the ventilator, the blood pressure monitor, and the machine pumping medicine into his body. He also had not started eating and was being fed through a PEG tube, and of course, he continued getting the seductive meds and antibiotics intravenously. He was under heavy antibiotics because they did not want him to contract any infections. He was still not cleared from the C. diff.

A team of doctors continued to monitor his condition—the pulmonary specialist, GI specialist, infectious disease doctor, cardiologist, and renal specialist.

He continued his medication, including sedatives and painkillers. All his medicines were administered intravenously except for one injection, which was to prevent blood clots because of his lack of movement and was being administered to his stomach.

Several tests were done to check the fluids oozing from his abdomen, but they could not find the source. They did a CT scan and fistula test and even tried to dye the formula they were feeding him to see if there was perforation or leakage in the intestines or stomach. All these tests did not give any indication of where the fluid was coming from. Since it was a lot, they had to use an ostomy bag and would empty and change it once or twice a day.

He was also being attended to by a speech pathologist, a physical therapist, and an occupational therapist. The physical therapists and occupational therapists were mostly working on a range of motions as Daniel was still very weak and his muscles had collapsed. After a couple of days, Daniel started learning to sit like a baby. Daniel never liked to be elevated, even when in bed. I used to wonder how he was feeling. He was in a lying position for many weeks, and I believe he was feeling dizzy or something, but he could not express himself. The nurses would ensure that he was put in an upright position for at least an hour or two. They would transfer him onto a jerry chair, but he would be restless the whole time, trying to get to a sleeping position. I would ask him how he was feeling, but he could not say anything.

After a couple of days in the hospital, the speech pathologist decided to do a swallow test to see whether Daniel could gradually start eating. He passed the test and started taking fluids. However, he could not take soft food as he was vomiting, so he continued to be fed through the PEG tube. I remember when he passed the test and was asked by the speech pathologist what the one thing he craved was. He said a banana. The speech pathologist was there for the trial, and she was the one feeding him. After two bites, he threw up everything. Henceforth, Daniel's stomach could not hold any food. The test he did was to ensure that when he drinks, the drink goes through the right way and does not go to the airways.

Daniel was slowly progressing, and now he would be put on the ventilator during the night. He still didn't seem to be aware of what was going on around him. After about ten days, he was moved to another ward because he seemed to be improving. Unfortunately, after a couple of days, he got pneumonia in his left lung, and immediately, they returned him to the ward he was in to monitor him closely.

He continued to be seen by a team of specialist doctors, including a pulmonologist, a gastroenterologist, an infectious disease specialist, a cardiologist, a renal specialist, and a general physician.

Daniel and I had a couple of visits to some doctor's offices away from the hospital. The ambulance rides were very emotional. Sitting with my son, watching him lie on a stretcher strapped, and not being able to help him broke my heart. I remember once when we went to see his GI; it was almost a half-hour drive, only to get there and be told that the hospital had made a mistake. The doctor was not working in that location on that particular day, so we went back to the Specialty Hospital without seeing anyone. Daniel's wound was still not healed; it was still oozing, so on our next visit, the GI decided that they should try to put a stent in his stomach, thinking that it would stop/block the oozing, the cause of which they had not known yet. Therefore, on November 6, I accompanied Daniel to the hospital next to Specialty Hospital for the procedure.

We continued to receive family members and friends coming out of state to visit. The day that was overwhelming for me and, I believe, for the hospital, too, was November 5, 2016, Labor Day, when family and friends visited. Carlos and family, Calvin and family, Mia, and Melanie and her husband, Kaden, visited from Minnesota; my cousin Anthony and his wife Nina visited from North Carolina; and my husband, came to see us from California. That afternoon, Daniel was wheeled out of the hospital building for the first time; his eyes could not stand the light. We took photos and videos, as it was a memorable occasion. I am sure the hospital staff was wondering, *Who is this patient who has such a big family?*

I remember the day my sister-in-law, Leah, surprised us with a visit. She had come to the United States but was in Columbus, Ohio. She decided to come for a day. That day, I had this feeling that I could not explain. Leah had made arrangements with Doreen without me knowing. I was overwhelmed by seeing her. Imagine seeing your family in such a situation. We went out for brunch; this was one of the rare moments I left Daniel alone in the hospital. It is still one of my most memorable days.

There were those friends who were regular visitors: Max and his fiancée, Irene. She would sometimes make samosas and mandazis (a kind of donut) and bring them to me. We were really blessed. Doreen, Harry, and their children were just around the corner and would come almost every day. Some of the friends continued to come and see us—Lynn and

Geoffrey, Enid, Tina, her mother, and her daughter Jackie. Enid and Tina would bring food during the weekend, which would last me for a whole week.

As it was with the other hospitals, I stayed with Daniel in the hospital. I was given a sleeping cot that had seen better days. It was very narrow, with a very thin mattress. The springs of the cot were poking when I lay down. Daniel's friend Karine and her fiancé, Ryan, came to visit, and when they saw it, they brought me a body pillow to ease the pressure off the springs from the cot. I was happy that I had a place to lie down compared to the rest of the hospitals, where I had to sleep on recliners.

At the hospital, some Kenyan nurses took care of me; they would check on me to make sure we were comfortable. I remember Maria used to make spiced tea and mandazi (our equivalent to donuts) and bring them to me when she came to work in the morning. She would tell me the evening before, "Mom, don't eat anything. I will bring you breakfast tomorrow." She had offered to take me shopping a couple of times, even though I was not comfortable leaving Daniel. Then one day, I decided to go with her to get some warm clothes for him since all his clothes were now oversized. I am ever grateful to God for sending me all these people to bless me during those trying moments.

Everly was among the people who also frequented to see Daniel. I know Everly through my sister-in-law. When she heard that Daniel was sick, she got in touch with me and came to see us. She would drive more than three hours to come see us, and she would always be bringing something she thought I would need at the hospital. She would visit with her son, Zion, nephew Talal, and husband, Sam.

After Daniel was weaned from the ventilator, we were advised that he was now ready to go to a rehabilitation facility. The case manager recommended two facilities and arranged for their staff to come and talk to us about their facility and the services they provided. I was inclined to move to a Rehabilitation Hospital. Harry came to pick me up from the Specialty Hospital to go and visit the facility before making a final decision. We did a tour of the place, and since Harry works in the medical field, he made some inquiries and was happy with the facility and the kind of service they provided. Moreover, the facility was new with new and updated equipment, and some of the nurses who worked there were working at the Specialty, so we were comforted by the fact that we would at least be seeing some familiar faces. The other advantage was that the rehabilitation hospital was close to Daniel's house, so it would be easy for me to go there in case I needed something.

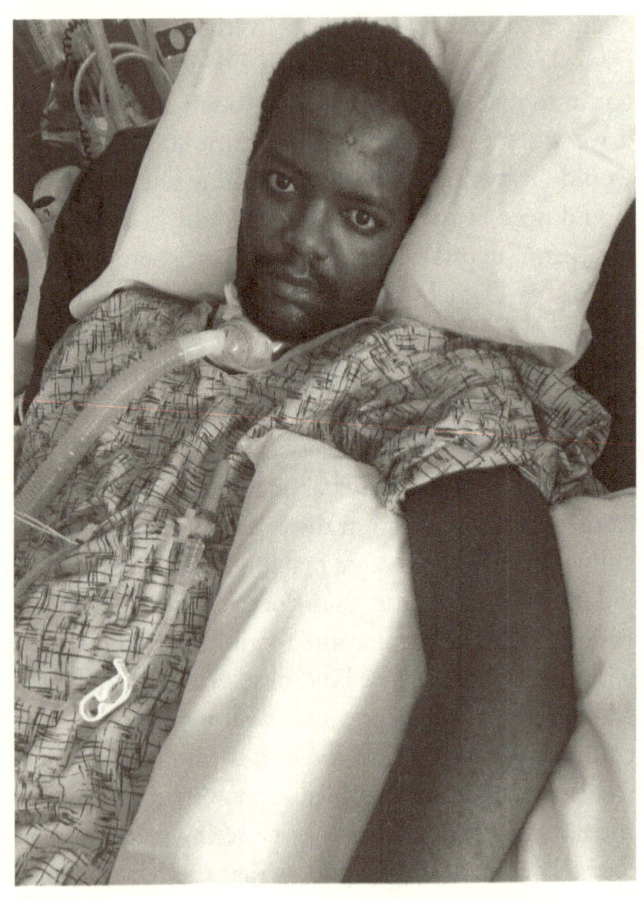

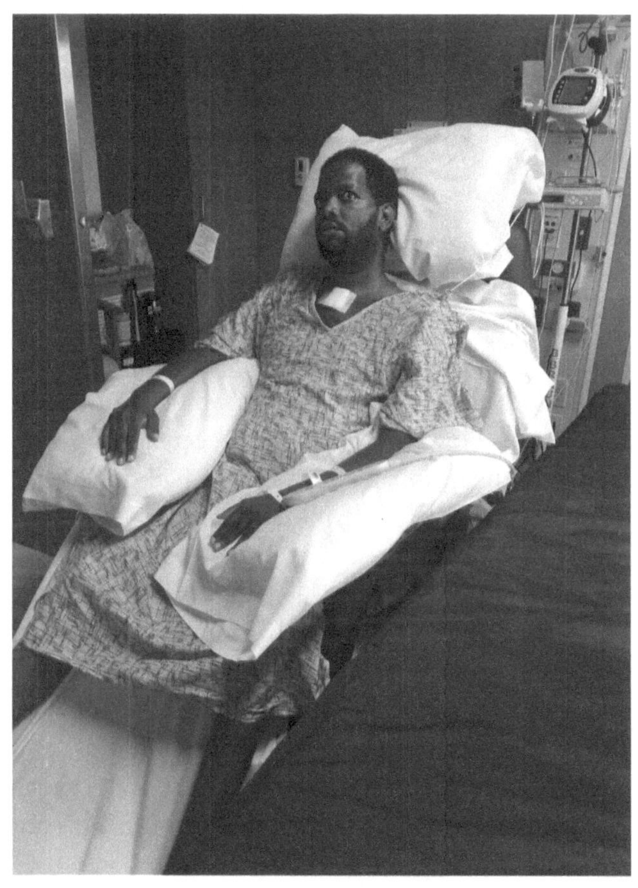

Rehabilitation Hospital

On September 16, we moved to the rehabilitation hospital. Again, we were blessed that Tess and Doreen were available to assist us in moving. Moving Daniel was not a big deal, as he would go into the ambulance. However, since I had been staying with Daniel in the hospital all this time, I had quite some belongings. My friends will tell you that wherever I am, I like my comfort, and therefore, I ended up having lots of stuff.

The rooms at the rehab hospital were bigger compared to those at Specialty Hospital. As we got Daniel settled, Doreen asked the nurse on duty to put an extra bed in the room for me. He was a bit hesitant and proposed to give me a cot, but Doreen insisted that they put a bed for me, saying, "My aunt has been sleeping on a recliner for three months." The nurse obliged, and I was offered a hospital bed.

For the first time in three months, I was able to sleep on a comfortable bed. Though I was comfortable, I had problems sleeping, first because I was restless. I could not let myself fall fast asleep in case Daniel needed my assistance. Also, the traffic of nurses and nursing assistants in and out of the room to check on Daniel, give him medicine, take specimens, and check on his tube feeding prevented me from sleeping deeply to some extent.

Daniel started proper therapy when we moved to the rehab hospital. He was doing physical therapy, occupational therapy, and speech therapy. He would do three hours, one hour for each therapy. Daniel started to learn how to sit, stand, walk, eat, brush his teeth, and write. He started from zero. I thank God that the hospital has very good facilities and therapists too. He was still being seen by a couple of doctors, including his brain doctor, and a nutritionist.

In the first few weeks, he did therapy in his room. The physical therapist would come and help him sit. He would be assisted to sit on the side of the bed and then gradually supported to stand using a walker. Slowly, he started standing and eventually practicing how to walk. He had a very good physical therapist, who would push him to the maximum. Daniel would be walking using the walker, and I would follow behind with a wheelchair in case he got tired and would want to sit.

After about a week, his physical therapist decided to leave the walker and support Daniel when walking. He practiced going up and down the stairs, going uphill and downhill. It was very taxing, but he persevered. Unfortunately, he got injured and could not work with Daniel anymore, and another therapist was assigned to him.

When Daniel started walking without a walker, he was walking like someone who had just recovered from a stroke; the rhythm was off. I remember watching him struggle to walk. It was very difficult for me, but I would encourage him by telling him he was doing great. Even as I am writing this, my eyes are tearing up. With time, he started walking better with the walker. They had him try out a walking stick, but he could not balance, and they felt it was safer for him to use the walker.

The speech therapist would also come every day for an hour to help feed him and assist him with reading and writing. I thank God that he had not lost his ability to write and read, though he was slow. Daniel was on tube feeding for the whole period he was at the rehab hospital because he could not eat much for him to get the required number of calories. He did not like eating and had no appetite, and whenever he ate, he would vomit. So at night, he would be put on the formula. He continued with the tube feeding even when we went home after being discharged.

While at the rehab, the occupational therapist had an hour with him every day and would normally help him brush his teeth, wash his face, and later take a shower. As he was getting better, we would go to the dining room for him to eat with other patients. At a certain stage, the therapist introduced him to preparing simple meals like soups.

When we were still at the rehabilitation hospital, I started going out and leaving Daniel for a few hours because his health had improved to some extent. Doreen was the one who insisted that I needed to get out for a change; otherwise, I would fall sick. They started picking me up to go to church on Sundays. But every time I was away, I would worry, and therefore, I made sure that I talked to the nurse on duty to take care of Daniel until I was back.

There was a revival program at the Lenexa Christian Center, which I attended from September 18–20. I was so blessed to partake in the revival program as I was able to attend one of the programs led by Dr. Bill Winston, whom I used to follow on social media. The programs were usually in the evening and ended at around eight to eight thirty. By then, the hospital did not allow visitors. I had to get special permission to come in after the hospital curfew. Though I worried about being away from my son for a couple of hours, I also felt spiritually fulfilled.

As I got more comfortable leaving Daniel alone for some time, I started attending Bible study on Thursdays. Doreen had made arrangements with one of the ladies in church to pick me up and drop me off at the rehab hospital. I thank God for all these people who were available and ready to support me during those difficult moments.

As Daniel got better and was able to sit, we would play games like building Lego blocks, and I would challenge him to construct something, or we would play catch. All these games were to help strengthen his motor skills. Whenever friends—Doreen, Tess, Max, and Irene—came to visit, they would also engage Daniel in a sort of challenge, like playing cards and catch. He would light up when Karine and Ryan visited; they would update him on sports, particularly football, and whatever was going on.

When Daniel was about to be discharged from the rehabilitation hospital, the therapists wanted to go see his house to make sure that it was compatible.

His house was a duplex, and there was a flight of stairs going into the house. As you entered the house, there were also a couple of stairs going up and down. They recommended some installations: a railing along the stairs going into the house and in his bathroom and a transfer chair for the bathtub. This was to avoid falling and also to allow him to move within the house.

We informed Daniel's landlord, and he made all the changes without any charges. I must say that Daniel's landlord was very understanding and cooperative during this period. I thank him from the depths of my heart.

God continued to bless us. We continued to have friends visit. Tess, Tina, her daughter Jade, and her mother would always bring food with them. Enid and Alaina would also bring food and fruits. Jane would come with fruits or cookies. I remember when we were still at the rehab hospital, Lina, a former colleague of Daniel from Kenya, called from the store and asked if I needed fruits. I told her that I had so much and that I didn't know what to do with them. She said she would buy me a blender to make smoothies. I told her that Daniel had one in the house that I could use. She insisted on buying one and said, "Mom, let me at least do something." I was so touched.

She got me the blender and brought it to the rehab hospital, and she came with her one-month-plus baby. What manner of love is that? It was even my first time meeting her. We were just speaking on the phone when she called to check on how Daniel was doing. She told me that when she worked with Daniel, he was very supportive and that she regarded him as a brother.

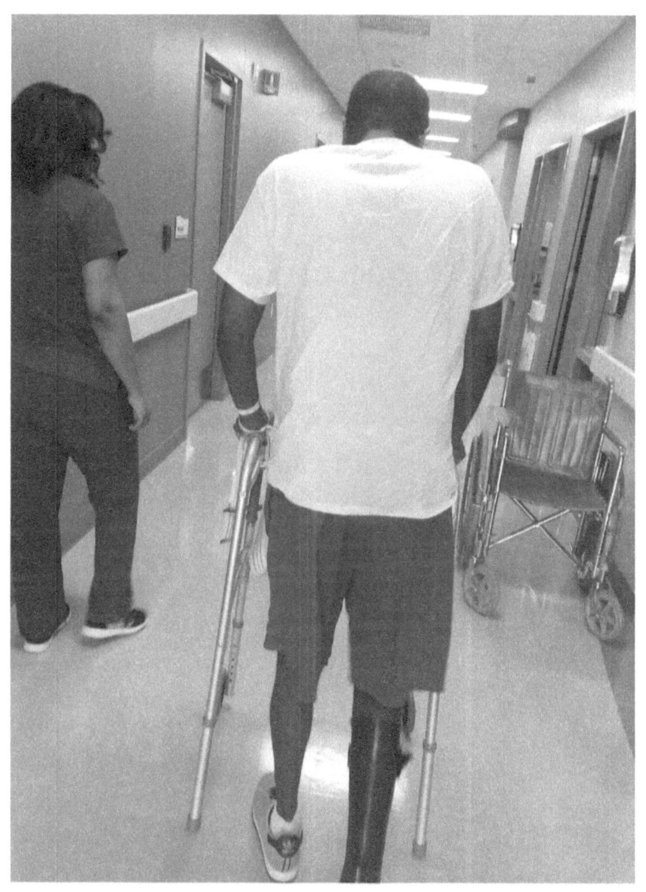

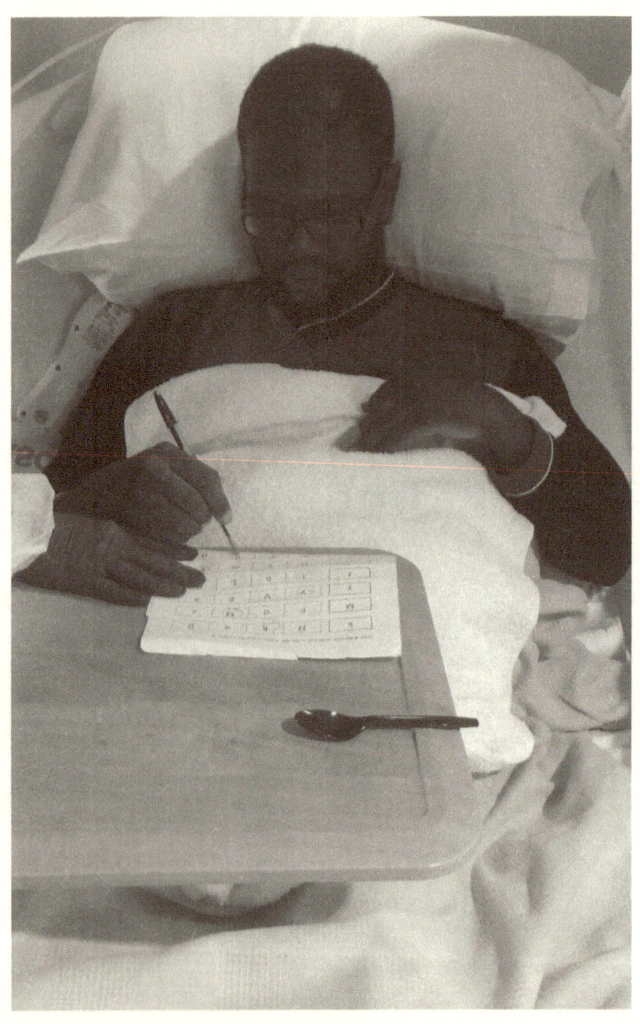

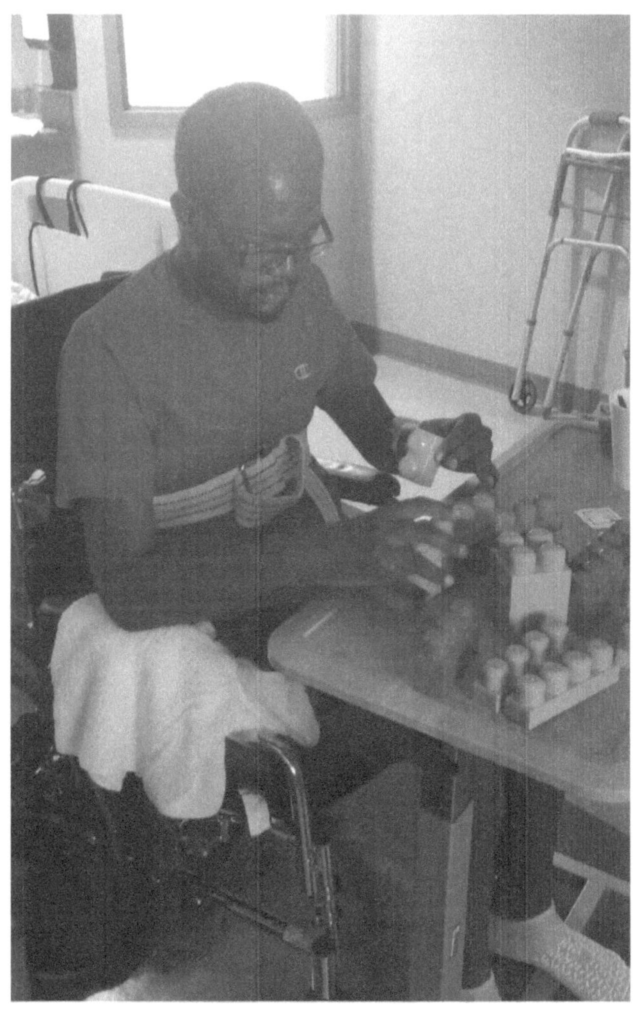

Back at Home

On October 25, 2016, Daniel was discharged from the Rehabilitation Hospital. We went home with his wound still not healed. He was still on tube feeding and was using a walker. It was not easy, but I thank God that I was able to manage with the support of friends and family.

Before we left the rehab hospital, the caseworker had made arrangements for a nurse to visit three times a week to take care of Daniel's wound. This really helped because she would come to check his vitals, dress his wound, and give advice in case there was an issue that needed medical attention. However, sometimes, in between her visits, Daniel would need his dressing changed. He still had the ostomy bag, and I would be obliged to change him because the dressing was leaking. It was not easy for me because I did not have the nerve to deal with wounds and all the medical issues attached. I also had to learn how to hook him on the tube-feeding pump at night.

Since he could not eat well, the nutritionist recommended that he needed an intake of a certain number of calories per day. The challenge was feeding at night. He was supposed to sleep in a certain position, at a ninety-degree elevation, to avoid choking, and he did not like that sleeping position. I, therefore, had to check on him at night all the time to make sure that he was sleeping in the prescribed position. Eating was a big challenge because he had no appetite. He was also taking Ensure to boost his nutrition; this was also a problem because he had gotten tired of it.

After Daniel was discharged from the rehab hospital, he was scheduled to continue with his therapy sessions three times a week: physical, occupational, and speech therapies. Since I wasn't driving, we used to take Uber to the hospital and would be there for three hours because he was doing an hour for each therapy session.

At home, once Daniel was at the upper level of the house, he would move from his bedroom to the bathroom, which was attached to his room using the railings. But he still needed assistance when taking a bath, particularly with the transfer, and I would therefore assist him. He used to spend most of the day in the living room, where he would be watching TV from morning to evening. His roommate Robby had bought him a recliner, which he really loved. He would recline on it, covered in the blue and white blanket that Lynn and Doreen bought him when he was in the hospital.

Before he came home, Doreen suggested that we go shopping and redecorate his room so that he could return to a new environment. Doreen, Tess, and I went shopping and got him new bedding, curtains, wall decor, and rugs (though this was put on the side and was not used because we were cautioned that rags would make him fall). We had also made some changes in his living room. Surprisingly, Daniel did not notice all the changes we made in his house.

When we got home, friends and family continued to support us. I didn't have to worry about going shopping. Tess would come once a week and take me shopping, and Enid would call from the grocery store when she was doing her grocery shopping and ask what I needed.

My bestie Christine, her son Timon, and grandchildren came to visit from Texas, as well as Max and his fiancée, Irene, after Daniel was discharged from the hospital. We spent the day with them and had a good time. Max, who lives in Missouri, and Irene, who lived in Omaha, Nebraska, would visit us frequently.

In November, I had to leave Daniel and travel to Sudan to have my Sudanese visa renewed. It was a very difficult decision for me to make because Daniel was still on tube feeding. He still had the ostomy bag and was not eating well. At that time, I was not sure if I wanted to go back to work and leave him. My friends and sisters in Darfur—May, Alaina, Natasha, Jane, Diana—convinced me to get the visa in case I wanted to return to Sudan. I made arrangements with his young brother Prince (from Houston, Texas) and cousin Dylan (from Columbus, Ohio) to come and stay with him for the period I would be away. I thank them for finding the time and agreeing to take on that responsibility.

I alerted my colleagues in our liaison office in Khartoum and sent them a letter from Daniel's doctor indicating that Daniel needed my care. They, therefore, attached the letter with my visa request to expedite the issuance of a visa and allow me to return to the United States as soon as possible. I got the visa and returned to Kansas within a week.

We continued going to his doctor's appointments. His wound healing very slowly was still a concern that remained. He was referred to a wound specialist, who recommended another surgery. My heart was heavy at the thought of him going for another surgery. When the wound specialist consulted Daniel's surgeon, he did not share the same opinion. He said that Daniel has had enough surgeries, and he would not recommend another one. He said that as long as there was an improvement, though slow, he would recommend that he continue with the treatment. The surgeon was troubled by the wound, though. He did some research and came across this steroid treatment. However, the treatment was very expensive, and he decided to abandon the idea. Daniel continued with the dressing and using the ostomy bag.

Most of Daniel's appointments were with his surgeon and the wound doctor at this point at the Regional Hospital. Every time we visited the hospital, I would ask him if it was okay to go to the ICU for the nurses and doctors who took care of him to see how he has improved. Daniel would always refuse. I think he was conscious of his limitations.

In early December, Daniel and I went to his workplace to follow up on his insurance and to see the prospects of him going back to work. We met with his director and the head of human resources.

By then, Daniel was walking on his own, though he was not strong enough. He still wanted to go back to his job as a CNA. We had a chat with them; however, he was not in a condition to work because of his memory. He was also not physically fit for the job.

Daniel continued to improve. Doreen and Harry would come to pick us up from Daniel's house to go to church and sometimes to spend time with the family. Then on Christmas Day, in 2016, they organized a get-together for a few close friends at their clubhouse. They cooked a lot of food. We ate, played games, and exchanged gifts, and the most exciting thing was to see Daniel participate. It was one of the best days since Daniel got sick. I am ever grateful to this family for taking us in as their own.

We were so blessed by the Tanzanian community in Kansas. On December 26, Tina invited us for lunch at her home. We had a good time with her daughter, Jackie, and her mother. I remember once, Jackie came to see Daniel in the hospital and brought him a handmade card and a small teddy bear, which he still has.

On New Year's Day, in 2017, we were invited for dinner at Enid and Alex's place. Sue and her boys and Enid's sister Camila and her daughter were also there. They prepared a lot of food; we ate and had a lot of fun.

Enid's and Sue's fathers worked with Daniel's father for many years, and they used to be friends. However, the three—that is, Enid, Sue, and Daniel—didn't know one another. But somehow, the girls felt they had a moral imperative, like family.

Tess, one of the people I am highly indebted to, invited us to her house on January 21, 2017. Tina and Jackie were also there. We had a wonderful time together. We ate, talked, and chilled. Jane was also very kind to us. She worked far from where we were in Kansas, but whenever she was in town, she would come to visit us and bring fruits along with her. She also invited us to her home for dinner before we left Kansas.

51

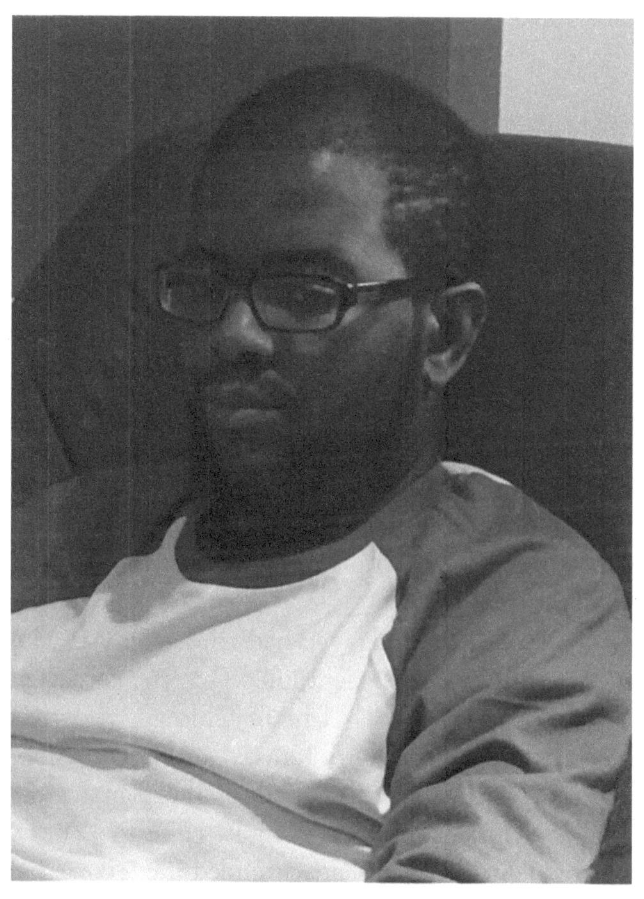

Thanksgiving

After Daniel had seen all his doctors and they were satisfied that he could travel to California, we started making plans for our move. One of the things I thought we should do was have a Thanksgiving service. This was to thank God and the Kansas community for the love and support they showered on us during the most difficult period of my life. Therefore, Doreen and I started planning and set the date for January 15, 2017.

Among the things we had to decide was who would officiate the occasion. Doreen contacted Pastors Charlotte and Clem in Chicago, and they were happy to travel to Kansas for the occasion. Doreen made reservations and all the plans at the Holiday Inn in Shawnee, Kansas, close to Lenexa, where Daniel lived. Friends attended the service and supported the event by bringing food and drinks. Doreen, Judy, Sue, Enid, and other ladies prepared food while Geoffrey decorated the hall. Some friends like Dr. Dora contributed to the renting of the hall for the service. Harry was the master of ceremonies, and Melanie played the piano for us. Everything was just perfect; I thank God for His favor.

The weather was very bad during that weekend. There was black ice; therefore, it was dangerous to drive. However, God made it possible for friends and the pastors to drive from Texas, Iowa, and Chicago. Christine, Timon, and his children traveled from Texas while Aaron and his family traveled from Iowa and Pastors Charlotte and Clem from Chicago. Many friends from Kansas and Missouri came for the service too. Daniel was very happy, especially when he saw his friends Kareen and Ryan. We had a wonderful time of prayer, thanksgiving, testimonies, and praise. Some friends who had not seen Daniel in a while were surprised to see him walking on his own and not in a wheelchair.

Packing Daniel's Stuff in Kansas

When we left Kansas with Daniel, we did not release his house immediately. So on March 3, I went back to Kansas to take care of Daniel's stuff and hand over the house to the landlord. It was a difficult task, as this was a full house with furniture, clothing, kitchen stuff, and other household items. Deciding what to do with everything was not easy. Before we went to California, Prince had come to Kansas to help with sorting out Daniel's documents and paperwork, which was a big relief.

Prior to leaving California for Kansas, I spoke to Doreen, Harry, and Max, so they were expecting me. Harry came to pick me up from the airport when I arrived and dropped me off at Daniel's house. Later, Doreen joined me to help with the packing. She also brought me food.

In Aiden's bedroom, all his baby clothes were still hung in the wardrobe the way they were since he went to Kenya with his mother in 2013. Then there was Daniel's room to sort out and the guest room, where Gail had left some stuff. The next morning, Max and Irene came by to help with sorting out and packing.

Max made several trips to the Salvation Army to drop off the items we had decided to donate. Irene and I moved from one room to the next, deciding what I should keep for Daniel. In fact, we ended up donating almost everything. Regarding furniture in the living room, dining room, and bedrooms, Daniel's landlord had found someone to take the furniture in both bedrooms, the TV sets, cabinets, and the dining table and chairs. The buyer came to the house, but I did not know how much money to ask for everything, so I asked Max to suggest a figure, which we agreed upon and gave him. The amount was not worth the items, but it meant less hassle. He even got a bonus of children's toys, bedding, and rugs for free.

This was one of the hardest and most painful moments of my life—to imagine that this was the end. Prince and I used to visit Daniel for holidays, and he would take days off to spend quality time with us. I had a lot of fond memories. Now thinking of my son, not knowing how his future was going to be, was very painful. I cried all the time. I do not know how to thank Max, Irene, Doreen, and Harry for standing by me during this time. Daniel was not even aware of what was going on. We had to make this hard decision on his behalf because we could no longer afford to pay rent for two homes in California and Kansas.

Moving to California

As he was getting better, Paul and I decided that it was expensive to maintain two homes: our home in California and Daniel's home in Kansas. I was still on leave of absence, so I was not earning a salary. So when the doctors were satisfied with his condition, we moved him to California to stay with us. He could not stay on his own because he still needed support. The other option was to leave him in Kansas and get someone to assist him. This would not give us peace; we would be worried all the time. His condition did not allow him to work, so he could not go back to his job.

I traveled with Daniel from Kansas to California on January 17, 2017, where Paul and I resided. Paul had made inquiries about all the assistance and specialists Daniel needed in California. By the time we left, his surgeon had removed the PEG tube for feeding on January 12, but his wound had not healed, and he also needed to continue with therapy.

First, we had to get Daniel's medical insurance in place because the one he had was from his workplace, and he could not use it since he had separated from them in December 2016. Once Paul was able to get an insurance policy for him, we were able to identify a primary care physician. His primary care physician referred him to a wound doctor, a cardiologist, a neurologist, and a mood doctor. We also had to find a therapy facility for him because he was required to continue with physical, occupational, and speech therapies. God was so faithful that we were able to settle him down within a short time, and he was able to continue with his treatment.

It took a little while to get the right facility for his therapy. Ultimately, we were referred to a Transitional Rehabilitation Center, where he started occupational, physical, and speech therapies. His program was twice a week from 8:30 a.m. to 3:00 p.m. They had different activities that were aimed at bringing him back to a normal life. They were taught how to prepare different simple dishes like soup, tacos, and pasta. The instructors would ask us to give him some petty cash for shopping. At this point, we had engaged a caretaker for him; her name was Elly.

Elly would come for six hours three times a week to assist him with reading, going for walks, doing some chores as part of his therapy, and also following up on his therapy activities.

As I mentioned earlier, I took leave of absence from work to be with my son. Though Daniel was now settled, I didn't feel like leaving him and going back to work. I wasn't sure how he would cope, and I felt it would also be a lot of responsibility for Paul as he was also working. In the meantime, I decided to enroll in a certified nursing assistant (CNA) course, which I started on March 27, 2017. This was plan B, just in case I could not go back to work. I completed the course and got certified. Elly was very instrumental, as she continued to take care of Daniel while I was attending classes. Elly came on the days that Daniel was not going to rehab and stayed from 8:00 a.m. to 2:00 p.m. when I came back from school.

Since Paul and I left early to go to work and school, we engaged a lady we knew who had a yellow cab, Rosie, to take Daniel to rehab and back. After a while, she said she could not continue with the service anymore. We then decided to ask Elly's husband, Gavin, if he could assist, and he gladly agreed. Elly and Garvin became part of our family.

I thank God that Daniel continued to get better and was coping well in his new environment. Then Paul and I finally decided that I could go back to work after eleven months of being away. However, we were prepared for me to come back anytime in case Daniel needed me back home.

I should confess that my friends played a big role in pushing me to return to work. I did not feel like leaving Daniel since he had not recovered fully and still needed supervision. Also, after having stayed with him for eleven months, it was difficult. Paul encouraged me and assured me that they would be okay. I was worried that it would be a lot of responsibility for him to go to work, take care of Daniel, and manage the house. I thank God that they managed well and that I did not have to worry when I was at work.

Paul was fully in charge of Daniel's doctor's appointments, medication, programs, and so forth, and they bonded very well.

Daniel's Progress

By the time I went back to work, Daniel had settled at the rehabilitation center, and he was getting better and better and gaining strength. He continued with the program for a year and a half.

After he completed his program at the Transitional Rehabilitation Center, he did a one-year program at the University of Southern California, Long Beach, where he attended speech therapy sessions for one year. By this time, Elly, his caretaker, had developed some health issues and could not take care of Daniel anymore, so she introduced her niece, Dina, to us, and we were happy to have her take over the role. Dina was the one taking him to his program, and she also supervised him and trained him to do chores in the house like laundry and cleaning his bathroom, as well as reading and writing. She would also take Daniel out occasionally.

After that, he joined the Acquired Brain Injury (ABI) program at the Coastline Community College in Newport, Orange County, for two years. The college was forty-five minutes away from Long Beach, where we lived, and it was difficult to find a regular ride to take him back and forth. We therefore introduced him to Uber. Paul went with him for the first couple of days, and after he was confident and comfortable, he started going by himself. He attended the program for two years, from January 2019 to December 2020. He graduated on May 26, 2021. At the ABI, he studied psychosocial, cognitive, and computer.

After completing the ABI program, Daniel decided he wanted to rest. Paul was in support of the idea, but I wanted him to be engaged because I knew that if he wasn't engaged in doing something, he would be watching TV the whole day. After six months, I decided to look for a program or someone to get him involved in something. I spoke to a friend who knew someone and gave me the contact information to reach out to. I did so, and Daniel started sessions, but they didn't last long because of some misunderstanding.

In August 2021, Daniel moved to Columbus, Ohio, where his cousin Penny and her husband,

Tom, invited him to stay with them. He was tired of staying in California because he did not have friends there. He said he wanted to move to Columbus, where his family is situated—Aunt Judy and family and his cousin Penny and husband, Tom, and Martin and family.

64

God's Favor in Daniel's Life

I thank God for His favor in Daniel's life. He placed "divine helpers" throughout his journey. I was not living in Kansas. I just used to visit, but I got great support from the Tanzanian and Kenyan communities in Kansas.

When Daniel was hospitalized at the Medical Center, the Tanzanian community had organized themselves, and the ladies would take turns cooking and bringing food to the hospital for me, Daniel's aunt, and our guests, so I didn't have to worry about our feeding. The Kenyan friends would bring water and soda and juice for whoever was visiting. Apart from taking care of our welfare, they would also advise on what to do to ensure Daniel's best medical care.

We received a lot of visitors who came to see him—those who live in Kansas and those who came from out of state. During the hospital visiting hours, our visitors filled the room. It was gratifying and humbling to see the attention we received. A special prayer line was started and dedicated to Daniel, and we would be praying every day at 8:00 p.m. When Daniel was transferred to the Regional Medical Center, friends and family did not abandon us; they continued coming to see us and bringing food and drinks. Then Daniel was moved to the Specialty Hospital, which was far from most of his friends. However, they were still committed to visiting and bringing food during the weekends.

Throughout Daniel's hospitalization, God blessed him with excellent doctors who were dedicated to saving his life. He also had very good and experienced caseworkers who wanted the best for him. The caseworkers at the Regional Hospital and at the Specialty Hospital recommended the best facilities. When we were ready to move to California, the caseworker at the Rehabilitation Hospital gave us the addresses of facilities we could look at when we arrived.

My travel from Darfur, Sudan, to Kansas to be with my son was by God's grace. The fact that I could afford the ticket and have the relevant documents to enter the United States was all the work of God. I believe that if I were not there on the night of July 11, 2016, my son would not have made it. Being there and God giving me the strength to challenge the doctors and the nurses to do what they were supposed to do was a game changer. I give God all the glory.

When we moved to California, God opened doors for Daniel's medical care and therapies: physical, occupational, and speech. Everywhere we went, we were well received, and the service was exemplary. When I went back to work, my cousin and best friend Ariana would come to my house and cook for Paul and Daniel food to last them for about two weeks. I am very grateful to her and her family for embracing my family.

I truly thank God for all the people who stood by me and my family during these very trying moments. Apart from those who were able to come to see us and support us in different ways, my family back in Tanzania—my dad, Owen and Leah, Joson and Josie, and Edmund and Joanna—were very supportive. I could see how my situation was bothering them, and they called me frequently to comfort me and see how they could help me. It was not easy for them being hundreds of miles away. My extended family, aunts, uncles, and cousins were also very supportive. My friends May, Alaina, Natasha, Diana, Ida, Sherley, and Addy; my fellowship partners and sisters Jocelyn, Becca, Claire, Marjorie, Madeline, Giselle, Bridget, Ashlyn, and Juliana; my church community; and colleagues at my workplace, especially those in my department, also rallied behind me and my family. Everyone in their own way showed their support and care, calling to see how we were fairing, praying for Daniel's healing, and making financial contributions. The support was overwhelming. I cannot mention everyone by name here, but I want to assure you all that I acknowledge and cherish you. My mom passed away in March 2004, and this is one of the times I really missed her. I wished she was there so I could cry my heart out to her. I did cry many times, but most of the time, I would hold myself not to worry my family and friends.

God has been with me throughout this journey and continues to open doors. He has never left or forsaken me. I will not pretend that it has been all rosy. Some days have been tough, but I always have family and friends who are there for me, and I am very grateful to God.

The intention of writing this book is to encourage other people going through the same experience not to give up and to believe and have faith in God. This will ease the pressure, knowing that there is a higher power who sees us and helps us to bear the burdens that we carry.

About the Author

Elizabeth is from Tanzania, in East Africa. She is a mother of two sons, Daniel and Philemon, and a grandmother of two, Jaxon and Aaron.

Elizabeth is a retired international civil servant. She is a DreamBuilder coach. Her passion is to empower the youth and inspire them to live the lives of their dream.

Elizabeth started her career as a foreign service officer at the Ministry of Foreign Affairs and International Cooperation of the United Republic of Tanzania, and during her career, she was privileged to work at the embassy of Tanzania in Addis Ababa. Following this, she joined the African Union where she worked with the mission in Darfur, Sudan. Later she joined the United Nations peacekeeping department and worked in the mission in Darfur and later in Somalia from where she retired.

Following her retirement, Elizabeth decided to pursue her passion for mentoring and coaching. Another passion she also enjoys is artwork and crafting, including epoxy resin art, and quilting.

When Elizabeth was growing up, her ambition was to become a journalist. However, she ended up studying political science, international relations, and diplomacy, hence her career with the foreign ministry, African Union, and the United Nations.

Meanwhile, the urge to write was still there, and when her son got sick in 2016, she decided to journal every experience they went through, and this is what culminated in the book *Daniel's Journey*. The book will take you through the challenging journey Elizabeth and her family and friends traversed and how God showed Himself every step of the way.